HOWTO LOVE AND ACHIEVE HEALTH AND HAPPINESS

Anthony Webster

ISBN: 978-1-962231-30-5 (Hardback Edition)
ISBN: 978-1-962231-31-2 (Paperback Edition)
ISBN: 978-1-962231-32-9 (Ebook Edition)

Published by: Crosswords Noble House
Cover Design by: Crosswords Noble House
Interior Design by: Crosswords Noble House

This book is a work of non-fiction. While efforts have been made to ensure accuracy, the author and publisher are not responsible for errors or interpretations. The advice herein may not suit every situation. Professional guidance should be sought as needed.

Book Ordering Information:
Crosswords Noble House
165 Broadway Suite 23rd Floor,
New York, NY 10006, USA

info@crosswordsnoblehouse.com
www.crosswords noblehouse.com
+1 347-741-8793

Printed in the United States of America

PROLOGUE

PROLOGUE

The first name that came to me for this book was 'THINGS WE DON'T TALK ENOUGH ABOUT and should do' and as you see I changed it to this slightly controversial title 'How to Love'. But if you think about it, you will eventually agree that it does make a lot of sense.

Perhaps I should explain. Saying that you love is one thing, showing how you love is another. Sometimes we say one thing and do something else. So to prove that we mean what we say we must behave in a manner consistent with our words. We love by showing that we care and by showing in all the small ways, respect, and consideration for others. The pursuit of a virtuous life is the answer to peaceful and harmonious living. These short, simple, and familiar maxims are topics for discussion, especially in the home where some parents feel embarrassed or reluctant to talk to their children about these matters, and in the schools where virtuous living is considered the private domain of each child. Everyday we see the outcome of such an approach – indiscipline, intolerance, and violence. Learning how to live harmoniously and peacefully with others must also be taught and learned.

Parents/Teachers:

Pick a topic and discuss one every day with your children/pupils. Make a point of discussing the virtues, it helps in character building and gives people ideals to aspire to, such as patience, humility, fortitude, honesty, abstention, contentment, courage, kindness, and discretion.

Discuss the vices that people are prone to and make them aware of the pitfalls of threading these paths such as laziness, envy, pride, quarrelsomeness, confusion, overindulgence, drugs, drunkenness, selfishness, discrimination, and intolerance.

Together we can make our world a better place to live in and we start doing this in the home. Some of us only speak to children when we must correct or scold them. Have good conversations with the young ones. They depend on us to show them the right way in a loving environment.

To love is to live
To live is to love.
Without love
Life is empty.
Do these things and you.
Love yourself and others.

If we observe these maxims, think before we speak, watch what we say, and know when to say it, in addition to adopting a loving healthy lifestyle, we should live longer happier lives and be considered wise and easy to get along with.

I have profited from these 'reminders to myself' as I like to call them, as that's exactly what they are, by rereading them anytime I get a chance. The reason is that we are prone to error and fall into unwise ways of thinking or reacting in ways that are not in our best interest, especially in spur-of-the-moment situations.

By reading these maxims and sharing them with others we help ourselves to remember that there is a wise, healthy, and constructive way to live. Reprint them and put them up in appropriate places, in the home, in schools, and in the workplace. You have my permission.

Anthony Webster
February 9, 2007

HOW TO LOVE YOURSELF AND OTHERS

Part 1

INTRODUCTION

Man will never be able to unravel the mystery of life but at least we can try to appreciate it by valuing it and making the most of it. We are given the gift of life which consists of soul, mind, and body by the Creator and placed on the planet to become real human beings – whole loving human beings. This awareness should assist us to behave in a manner consistent with someone who has been given the awesome responsibility of taking care of such a wonderful gift. We do this first by loving and valuing ourselves. We love and value ourselves by following rules and principles which enable us to live a happy life – a life filled with purpose, caring, sincerity, and serenity. There is nothing that can compare with such an achievement. If you have seen the movies 'The Six Million Dollar Man' and 'Robocop', you would realize that these are examples of the wonders of science in the quest to remake man or at least parts of him to enable man's body to function efficiently after an accident. They pale in comparison with the wonders of nature and the miracle of the human body. Here is one reason to love yourself; we are caretakers of the most magnificent and intricate piece of equipment created – the human body which of course can only function if it has life, just as a vehicle can only function if it has a driver. Consider your soul (your life force) as the driver and your body as a priceless piece of equipment, loaned to you for your use and safekeeping for your life journey. Alas, some of us value and take greater care of our vehicles than of ourselves. Probably it's a good thing that human beings are not always taken up in how wonderful they are made as we may be tempted to stand around admiring ourselves all day.

I hope that I will be able to convince you that what matters most is that you take responsibility for these gifts seriously, enjoy them, take the best possible care of them, and live in peaceful coexistence with others.

Chapter 2 - The General Guidelines for Peaceful and Harmonious Living shows us how to love ourselves.

GENERAL GUIDELINES FOR PEACEFUL AND HARMONIOUS LIVING

GENERAL GUIDELINES FOR PEACEFUL AND HARMONIOUS LIVING

- Respect authority
- Get an education
- Invest in Lifelong Learning (keep on learning all your life)
- Accept responsibility for your life and your actions
- Develop your talents
- Use your initiative
- Practice self-control
- Enjoy your life
- Help others
- Be considerate
- Try understanding and appreciation rather than criticizing
- Try to live by the highest principles

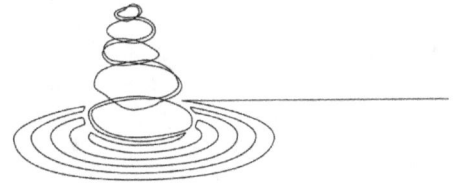

GENERAL GUIDELINES FOR PEACEFUL AND HARMONIOUS LIVING AT HOME

GENERAL GUIDELINES FOR PEACEFUL AND HARMONIOUS LIVING AT HOME

- Respect your parents
- Don't waste time
- Don't use other people's property without asking
- Put things back after using them
- Help around the house without being asked
- Keep a clean scene
- Attend to allocated chores
- Find out / Ask before accusing
- Discuss / Have conversations; don't argue
- When you earn, contribute to the home
- Train your children
- Be disciplined
- Children: get parents' permission first on key issues e.g., staying out late, giving away household items, inviting friends home, etc.

IDEALS AND PRINCIPLES FOR PEACEFUL AND HARMONIOUS LIVING IN THE OFFICE

IDEALS AND PRINCIPLES FOR PEACEFUL AND HARMONIOUS LIVING IN THE OFFICE

- Respect everyone
- Don't Gossip
- Organize/manage your time
- Give an honest day's work for an honest day's pay
- Look after the total well-being of employees
- Support your boss
- Be a team player
- Keep learning
- Give your best to your organization/employer

IDEALS AND PRINCIPLES FOR PEACEFUL AND HARMONIOUS LIVING IN PUBLIC

IDEALS AND PRINCIPLES FOR PEACEFUL AND HARMONIOUS LIVING IN PUBLIC

- Respect everyone
- Obey road safety rules
- Be considerate
- Give others a chance
- Don't obstruct the pavement or the roadway
- Greet others; return greetings
- Don't interfere in other people's business
- Help in any way you can
- Think before you speak/act
- Don't get into altercations; walk away (don't argue with an arguer) (Admit if you are wrong and if necessary apologize)
- Live and let live
- Leave good enough alone (don't do things that will make matters worse).

EPILOGUE

EPILOGUE

I make no excuse for the brevity of this book, for it is also written with the hope of getting those who as a rule do not like or want to read, to read it. I have been encouraged to make this book longer, but I resisted for two reasons: the one given above and the other—the hope that if you do not understand anything in it, it would encourage 'good' talk, conversation, questions, and discussion. "Things we don't TALK ENOUGH about but should do!" If you have read from the beginning and reached this far, I have achieved my first goal. If you had sought explanations or discussed anything contained within, I would have achieved my second goal.

This book will not be complete if I omit the words of the great teacher and exemplar of how to love—Jesus Christ. The coming of Christ signaled a new dispensation. While the Ten Commandments will forever remain a guide to humanity for the rules of right conduct, Jesus reduced/summed up these commandments to two:

- *Thou shalt love the Lord thy God with thy whole heart, thy whole soul, thy whole mind, and thy whole strength.*
- *Thou shalt love thy neighbor as thyself.*

This is not a book on religion, but it is a book about the second commandment—loving yourself and your neighbor, which is the key to peace on the planet.

Finally, remember that love is not just about a dry observation of these guidelines. Remember always that love comes from the heart, and we need always to listen to our heart. Loving is about being observant of the need for love and affection in others and fulfilling them to the best of our ability.

THINGS WE DON'T TALK ABOUT ENOUGH
And should do.

We are familiar with every single ideal and principle outlined herein, but because we don't talk about them enough, value them, and promote them, we fail to practice, remember, and teach them to our children. These are topics for everyday discussion with all children to encourage them to be noble citizens in a more beautiful world. We need to remind our children of the benefits to themselves of living virtuous lives. The media spreads the message mostly of vice and crime because that is what sells. Here is our opportunity to counteract this influence and make a positive contribution to the young lives for which we are responsible.

LIFELINES

Part 2

*Dedicated to my wife Rita who played such a
wonderful role in my life*

PROLOGUE

PROLOGUE

I believe that there are some universal laws, not much unlike the laws of physics and chemistry, that apply to human behavior. Probably not as exact, but usually reliable. They are more like cause and effect. Most of us are aware of most of them as we usually garner them from experiential learning and they help us to succeed in life and keep out of trouble. They can be as profound as "Chance favours a prepared mind" or as practical as "Choose your friends". There are a few that elude us and the lack of this knowledge gives us no end of grief in coping with some situations in life.

I have endeavored to reveal some of these secrets to you in Lifelines. They do not deal with all situations you may encounter, but they give you an idea of the approaches you could adopt in dealing with them. Most of the areas that give insight into human behavior and how we relate to others can be found in the study of psychology and sociology. But the average person does not go to these lengths to understand and deal with the business of everyday living. Most of them just wing it.

Here are a few pointers for us wingers:

- This book is not for the very young or the squeamish as it contains some very choice language, which if I had deleted would have watered down the message I am trying to convey.
- Consider this book a manual for those who wish to broaden their minds and the internal management

of their thoughts and emotions in their encounters with all types of people.

These are thoughts garnered from every facet of my readings and learnings. Where I have the sources, I have acknowledged them, but I am sure I have not always been able to do so. To those from whom I borrowed their wisdom without acknowledgment, I thank them most sincerely for allowing me to share it with the world.

Anthony Webster

1. Live each day reverently.

2. Real joy comes not from ease or riches or from the praise of men, but from doing something worthwhile.

3. The only medicine for suffering, crime, and all the woes of mankind is wisdom.

4. The main thing is to keep the main thing the main thing. For any person in an important position, be it religious or secular, the main thing to remember is: *"The fear of the Lord is the beginning of wisdom"*.

5. *The only thing necessary for evil to triumph is for good men to do nothing.*

    - Edmund Burke

6. If you want to improve you've got to be prepared to look foolish.

7. The Greeks never wrote obituaries. When a man died they simply asked 'Did he have passion?'

8. *There is no such thing as a moral or immoral life. Life is well lived or badly lived, that is all.*

    - Oscar Wilde

9. Full many a flower is born to blush unseen.

    - Gray 1751

10. Don't make little things a problem. Don't be petty. Rise above little things. Use the common expressions in regular use in these times to help you put the

situation in its proper perspective: *'small thing'*, *'whatever'*. Let some big thing takeover your life.

11. Walk softly, but carry a big stick. Winston Churchill

12. *'Be still and know that I am God'*; listen to the still small voice.

13. Achieve effortlessly, do less and achieve more, work smarter not harder. Hard work may not necessarily be good work if done at the wrong time. Timing is of paramount importance. *"He labours in vain who builds the house, if the Lord does not build the house"*.

14. Learn from yourself. See how you react. Most likely people may react the same way you do. *(Just remember we are not all alike.)* Use this knowledge in your dealings with people. It may teach you how to get along with them, influence or ignore them.

15. Don't think of death as the end, just as cutting down on your expenses.

16. Sex; is not the quantity so much as the quality. You and your partner must decide just how much is enough to keep you both happy.

17. Don't allow anyone to make you feel inferior. Remember always that you have your worth and nobody can take that away from you.

18. Carpe diem—seize the day; get a piece of the action while you can.

19. You must do the best with what you have while you have it.

20. Better discrete than eloquent.

21. *I am not an optimist, because I am not sure that everything ends well. Nor am I a pessimist because I am not sure that everything ends badly. I just carry hope in my heart. Hope is a feeling that life and work have meaning. You either have it or you don't, regardless of the state of the world that surrounds you. Life without hope is an empty, boring, and useless life. I cannot imagine that I could strive for something if I did not carry hope in me. I am thankful to God for this gift. It is as big a gift as life itself.*

   - Václav Havel

22. Sometimes you may have to get on like an ass because braying may be the only language some people understand.

23. As you go through life you are sure to meet many assholes; don't let them influence you, try not to imitate them.

24. When there is no plausible explanation for some people's behavior, consider 'stupidity' as a possible explanation. It will help us tremendously in our day-to-day affairs if we remember that people are not stupid deliberately. It should help us to be patient and understanding. There may be many things we may be able to fix in life but unfortunately, we can't fix stupid.

25. When you deal with people who are *"good for themselves"* you must be *"better for yourself"*.

26. Remember that your automatic response to a situation may not always be the correct one. Stop and think. It's one thing we can never stop doing—thinking.

27. Recognize your human needs and fulfill them within the framework of society. Respect the fabric and framework of society, live within them, or live to regret it; observe the laws of the land.

28. Educate yourself; get a profession or learn a trade. It is the most recognized and proven method of attaining a comfortable lifestyle.

29. Take responsibility for your health, physical, mental, and spiritual.

30. We are more than what we have made ourselves, but we should be able to unmake that which we made ourselves into if it is not working for us.

31. Accept your limitations; you may not be able to be all things to all men.

32. I will not be a thoughtless individual whose personality, approach to life, or philosophy is molded in the cast of negative and destructive reactions to the words of others which are thrown in my way for the main purpose of aggravating me, relieving their frustrations, or venting their pitiful fury. May I never allow myself to be swayed by the wind of words uttered merely to infuriate or hurt me. I refuse to be a puppet to the braying of every ass, moved by these noises to utter similar ones. *"Bray on brother, the chip you carry on your shoulder has made you into a beast of burden".*

33. Learn when to say no. Some people may expect miracles from you.

34. *Do just once what others say you can't do, and you will never pay attention to their limitations again.*

   - James R. Cook

35. Never take advantage of another.

36. Help in any way you can.

37. Don't judge; people have both good and bad qualities; work to improve yourself.

38. Have an open mind.

39. Be calm, be a balm.

40. Pay attention to the management of your own life and business affairs; recognize when you need help and seek it.

41. Choose your friends.

42. When thine eye is single thy whole body will be light.

43. While words can elevate, encourage, and ennoble, they can also cause trouble and confusion. Mind your words. To speak without thinking is stupidity.

44. *You've got to write your own story whether you are afraid or not.*

   - Lord of Light

45. The best defense is a good offense.

46. You can be a blessing, a trial, or a tribulation to others. It's your choice. It will all work for others. It's only when you are a blessing it will work for you. Be a blessing!

47. Recognize your gifts; appreciate and make full use of them lest they be taken from you. For instance, if you stop whistling or singing, eventually you will be unable to do it well.

48. Most of us have some capacity to learn but not all of us have the inclination. Those who are blessed with the inclination and capacity to acquire knowledge may do so for their own enlightenment or to assist others, although it is most difficult to teach those who do not want to learn by listening or reading. We all must fulfill our own destiny. The knowledge that you acquire may be for your requirement and enlightenment, not necessarily to share with others, unless that is your path. Some have neither the inclination nor the capacity, that is their path.

49. Stop and take note of where you are and where you are headed. To lay your anxieties to rest, you need a detached, balanced state of mind. Slow down and take a deep breath. Rush ahead blindly and you will not achieve the desired result.

50. You may not always be able to control the reaction or behavior of people with whom you must associate. Carefully choose the times for the discussion of sensitive matters that people may not want to hear. Remember that they don't have to

agree with you and on some occasions, they may react unpleasantly. If you are not prepared to deal with such reactions, then your alternative would be to avoid the discussion. If you feel it absolutely necessary to discuss the matter, be prepared for negative reactions and to deal with them. Dealing with them can be tricky. So, think beforehand and prepare yourself before you deal with sensitive matters or people so that the matter does not escalate into a full-blown argument. Always try to keep these confrontations brief. They tend to be drawn out as people try to prove their innocence whether they are guilty or not.

51. Don't let your situation get you down.

52. Regardless of what we do to each other, God is taking care of all of us. Remember to pray first, not as a last resort; and that when you pray you should also listen.

53. The real secret is becoming more childlike every day.

54. Your enemy is your Buddha.

55. It's not the years that counts, it's the moments.

56. Nobility is not a birthright, it's defined by one's actions.

57. Do you have the courage of your convictions?

58. Don't promise what you can't deliver.

59. There are days when you need to sin bravely and make trade-offs between one goal and another.

60. Reserve has an aspect of divinity about it.

61. Each of us has a path. A path does not lead to nowhere. Whatever happens in our lives prepares us for the future, each individual future. Nothing is revealed before its time.

62. Don't argue with an arguer. Most times the quickest way to end an argument is to admit when you are wrong.

63. Ego—the spanner in the works against successful agreements.

64. People can't always help being the way they are, and if they have annoying habits, they may either not know, not care, or don't see the need to change. If we must be around them, we just have to learn to ignore those behaviors and idiosyncrasies that annoy us.

65. A good part of our difficulty as we go about the business of living lies in our views of the nature of reality, of relationships, of self, and of our prescribed roles. We continually confuse reality— 'how things are' with our perception of 'how they should be'. 'How things are' may not always be to our liking. We must decide whether we should accept the status quo or do something about it if we can. This decision is key to our balance and sanity. The decision can be summed up very simply. 'Deal with it or accept it'. There are days when we need to make trade-offs between one good and another. The alternatives, not very attractive ones are to choose the path of complaining, whining, blaming

others, or not caring. It helps if you realize that all the previous are learned behaviors. Unlearn them. Learn more constructive behavior. Try dealing with it or accepting it! It's in your best interest.

66. Do not be afraid to give willingly, there is no loss in the divine mind. Sometimes whatever you give may come back to you tenfold. And do not look to the receiver of our gifts to return the favor. God is the source of our supply. Remember that whatever we have is what we have received. We sometimes play a part in creating it. It was given to us for our use. What is important is how we use it. Sometimes it is better to keep what you have for your use if you need it more than others. Be aware also that giving and receiving create obligations.

67. What must go, should go.

68. In your patience, you will win your soul.

69. Chance favors a prepared mind.

70. *When we really love ourselves, everything in our life works.*

   - Louise Hay

71. Let love be your guide, love for yourself involves loving your neighbour.

72. While it is obvious that we do not know it all, we frequently behave as if we do. When you stack up visceral emotion against reason, emotion usually wins. There will be times when we will have discussions with others who feel that they

are right, and you know that you are right. Try to remember that the other person may be thinking and feeling the same way as you do. In situations like these, you may have to agree to disagree... and live to fight another day.

73. The way of God is different from the ways of man. Don't rely on any one person to fill your need for love and affection. Remember that most do not 'love' you for who you are but for what you can do for them. A stranger may care more than family and friends. When you find someone who loves you for yourself, cherish them, it's a rare treasure and a precious gift from God. Man's quest for happiness lies in finding mutual satisfaction. There is always the need for discretion and caring. Follow your conscience, and let God be your guiding light. *'Thou wilt keep him in perfect peace whose mind is stayed on thee'.*

74. Unless it is your civic duty or responsibility, one of the most important lessons you must learn in life is how to or how not to correct others and whom to correct. Not having this knowledge can cause all kinds of confusion and disharmony in your life. Just leave some people alone to go their own way *(this does not apply to those in your care).* Remember that during the lifetime of Socrates and Jesus that was one of the reasons they were unpopular and condemned to death, but this was their path. Is it yours?

75. Sometimes all that is needed is an effort of will, intention, and acceptance. The battle is within. While we all have to help one another, we are exactly where we need to be. Thus, while in our

eyes it may seem to be, no individual's lot is worse than another. We just don't know all the reasons why they are where they are, and what they have to work out in their lives.

76. Wisdom is knowing what to do in most situations to achieve a happy outcome or an optimum solution. Wisdom is knowing how to use knowledge to your benefit. Hence the importance of acquiring knowledge which is the foundation of wisdom. Do not spend all of your time listening to the news, while it may be good entertainment, it adds nothing of lasting value to your life. Have a predisposition for wisdom, health, wealth, and happiness. Expecting it is conducive to achieving it.

77. Negotiation is a survival tool for us all. When you use it, think not only of winning at all costs. Try for a win-win situation, thinking not only of the present but the future as well.

78. A good leader must listen to his followers but should not be unduly influenced by strong partisan arguments. His decision must be for the good of the majority.

79. Purify your system, and your blood; get rid of hate and the desire for revenge. Top it off with the tonic of forgiveness and you will fly. Acknowledge your wrongdoing and forgive yourself as well. This is the beginning of the attainment of joy in your life—the joy of living.

80. Let your heart be right with God. Do house cleaning. Ask yourself. Whom do I hate? ... and stop hating

them. Whom have I not forgiven? ... and forgive them. Peace and goodwill will follow.

81. One of the ways of achieving greater awareness or consciousness is to ask yourself these questions: Why am I doing this thing? Who am I doing this for? The honest answers may surprise you.

82. *Enjoy when you can, and endure when you must.*

- Johann Wolfgang von Goethe

83. If you keep doing what you have always done, you will keep getting what you have always got.

84. Don't pine for the past, some things never repeat themselves; remember the good memories with joy; try to forget the bad times and thank God that they are gone. Learn from all your experiences, good and bad.

85. *When really turning toward truth, you will feel truth turning toward you.*

- Sherman Baksh

86. *Life can be understood only by looking behind but can be lived only by looking ahead.*

- Sozen Kierkegaard

87. *"There are no exact guidelines. There are probably no guidelines at all. The only thing I can recommend at this stage is a sense of humor, an ability to see things in their ridiculous and absurd dimensions, to laugh at others and at ourselves, a sense of irony regarding everything that calls out for parody in this world.*

In other words, I can only recommend perspective and distance. Awareness of all the most dangerous kinds of vanity, both in others and in ourselves. A good mind. A modest certainty about the meaning of things. Gratitude for the gift of life and the courage to take responsibility for it. Vigilance of spirit."

- Havel—1999

88.   *"It has been our absolutely basic historical experience that, in the long run, the only thing that can be truly successful and meaningful politically must first and foremost—that is, before it has taken any political form at all—be a proper and adequate response to the fundamental moral dilemmas of the time, or an expression of respect for the imperatives of the moral order bequeathed to us by our culture. It is a very clear understanding that the only kind of politics that truly makes sense is one that is guided by conscience."*

- Havel in 1999

89. If you find yourself in a pickle of some sort today, don't just experience this situation. Use it mindfully to move yourself closer to the person you want to be. When all is said and done, the opportunity for life-altering change is never more available to you than when you are right smack in the middle of one of life's firestorms.

90. You will never become who you want to be by remaining who you are! It's such an apt expression because it cuts right to the chase and puts the

responsibility for change right where it belongs … in your hands! If you want a different life, a healthier body, or a better job, it won't happen until YOU make it happen.

91. The end of one thing is **ALWAYS** the beginning of something else. Life is truly amazing in that way. Heartache, crisis, and disappointment touch all of us on occasion, but those who remain optimistic and find future happiness are those who deal with these situations the best. It's not what happens to you … it's how you respond that creates the kind of life that you live. When all is said and done, happiness, optimism, and peace of mind are all tied to your perspective. So, whether it's a job you've lost, a relationship that has turned sour, or something else that has changed dramatically in your life, remember: The end of one thing is ALWAYS the beginning of something else. What that "something else" becomes is entirely of your making. Stop looking back because your future is definitely not behind you. It's straight ahead!

92. Learn about human nature; learn about yourself. When we learn the right things about how to live and deal with situations and we practice it, life becomes easier. When we see things from their right perspective, it's like achieving nirvana. Everybody helps if we only take the time to really listen. It may not seem to make sense at the time and we may need to pick sense out of nonsense. But the effort may be worth it and it will always be to our advantage.

93. Rise above peoples' faults. It's their lives.

94. *It is not death that man should fear, but he should fear never beginning to live.*

   - Marcus Aurelius

95. *And in the end, it's not the years in your life that count. It's the life in your years.*

   - Abraham Lincoln

96. Don't get so busy making a living that you forget to make a living! Nobody on their deathbed ever wishes that they would have spent more time at work! Balance is the key to a happy and healthy life.

97. Make today the day you begin living in the present and start letting the past become what it is ... history!

98. Don't take your time on this earth for granted, love those close to you with more passion and be mindful of the wonderful opportunity you have each day to live your life and pursue your dreams. Old age is not guaranteed to anyone, no matter who you are or how healthy you live. Tragic incidents in life remind us to reshuffle the playing cards in our personal deck of life and reprioritize what's important to us. Start living the life you dream about today because nobody is guaranteed a tomorrow! Appreciate the wonder of life and all it has to offer as living within space and time is the ultimate adventure.

99. Enjoy all of the living beings around you who contribute to your life because one day illness, accident, or time will inevitably claim them. But, as the late Beatle George Harrison once wrote, all

things must pass. Personal incidents in our lives remind and encourage us to enjoy those around us more. Be sure to demonstrate your love for those you care about, and appreciate the pets and people who make up the daily fabric of your life because eventually, all things must pass. Personal incidents in our lives, like accidents that may have been traumatic or tragic, also force us to ask ourselves some fundamental questions like, *"Time is so precious—am I using it wisely?"* *"I have behaved a certain way for nearly all my life—should I change this behavior now?"* These questions help you to evaluate how you spend your time and whether you should be making changes in your life.

100. *"Once man begins to think about the mystery of his life and the links connecting him with the life that fills the world, he cannot but accept, for his own life and all other life that surrounds him, the principle of Reverence for Life. He will act according to this principle of the ethical affirmation of Life in everything he does. His life will become in every respect more difficult than if he lived for himself, but at the same time, it will be richer, more beautiful, and happier. It will become, instead of mere living, a genuine experience of life."*

From "Out of My Life and Thought" by Albert Schweitzer.

101. Receive gratefully and graciously
Ask, you may receive Gifts that cannot be demanded. Though your needs may be great No one person can fulfill them all. If you are to keep those who share what they can with you Do not

ask for more than they can give. For whatever little they may have been capable of sharing with you That too you may lose. Accept graciously whatever gift they bring It may only be an idea that could change your life. Do not impose on the bearer of gifts All of your life's burdens. They may have been sent to you for only one reason To solve one problem. Differentiate between fighting for what is rightfully yours And what is rightfully theirs To have, hold, and keep Or to share with you.

HEALTH AND HAPPINESS

Part 3

CONTENTS

1

STAYING HAPPY IS YOUR OWN RESPONSIBILITY

There are many "happiness areas" in our life. Let's however consider the human condition; there are things we have to do practically everyday which we take for granted. Brush our teeth, bathe, shave, make up, dress, eat, go to work etc. This is normal. Some of us actually enjoy doing some of these things. It's no big deal. To those of us who don't enjoy these everyday things, we thank God that we are creatures of habit.

Some of us however face some unfortunate situations in our lives e.g. having to deal with disagreeable people e.g. people who quarrel, nag, and find fault with everything. If, happily, we do not fall into any of those categories and we have to deal with such people we quickly realize that, mainly, happiness in our lives come from living with people who are nice to be with and that if we want people to be nice to us, it helps a whole lot if we are nice to them. It's the age old adage, *"Do unto others as you would have others do unto you"*. And it usually works.

Where we have problems achieving this bit of comfort in our lives its usually when we are stuck with people who don't believe in the adage, who don't work at it and don't care about other people's feelings. If they feel miserable, they will make others feel miserable. Misery love company. And that goes for all of us. We all need people to put up with us when we are not in the best of moods. It's dealing with selfishness that's the real problem.

So what's the solution. First of all, we should try to be people that other people can be comfortable with. And if we succeed in this and others are not following our example, we have to develop skills to keep our equilibrium i.e. to put up with selfish people who make our lives miserable. Mostly we may just have to be patient and don't do or say anything to make matters worse. If it's your lifemate, you may just have to ride out these situations the best way you know how. You should know them better than anybody else and should know what works best.

Here's another hint. Anytime anything upsets you, don't let that one thing take over your life, especially if its trivial. If it's important, you will have to give it the attention it deserves and deal with it as best as you can. If it's trivial, try and remember that it is just one incident. Don't dwell on it, disentangle yourself and move on to the other happiness areas of your life. Remember, it's your life, take responsibility for your happiness.

2

TOP 10 HEALTHIEST FOODS

There are tons of healthy foods, but not every food is considered Super healthy food. I will share a list of the healthiest food that we can eat these days.

Here are the Top healthiest foods you can eat:

1. WALNUTS

The number of antioxidants this nut has is just mind-blowing, there is a reason for it to be one of the healthiest food in the world, it is rich in omega-3 fatty acids, the combination of healthy fats, protein, and fiber in walnuts helps to increase satisfaction and fullness.

Benefits:

- Heart health
- Weight management
- Bone health

2. SPINACH

Spinach is considered to be a superfood, it is filled with tons of nutritional benefits. Almost every green food is good for health, but spinach is on the top of that list. Spinach is important for your bone health, hair and skin as it is filled with vitamins, minerals, and iron. The secret of Popeye strength.

Benefits:

- Good For Diabetic patients
- Prevents Asthma
- Prevents Cancer
- Bone Health
- Good For Digestive issues

3. BLACK BEANS

Black beans as also known as turtle beans due to their appearance. It is classified as legumes, there are other legumes such as lentils, peas, and peanuts. Black beans are known for their high fiber and protein content. They contain many nutrients that are beneficial for your health.

Benefits:

- Bone Health
- Good for diabetes
- Good For heart health
- Weight Loss

4. DARK CHOCOLATE

You might have heard that chocolate is not good for you, well turns out it's not. Keep in mind that I am only talking about natural dark chocolate, not those sugar-filled fake chocolates. Dark chocolates are rich in minerals that are vital for your health. It contains zinc, magnesium, and iron. Cocoa in dark chocolate has antioxidants in them that provide various health benefits.

Benefits:

- Prevents Cancer
- Prevents Eye disease
- Reduces heart disease
- Beneficial for Alzheimer's Disease

According to recent research, chocolate contains more antioxidants, gram-for-gram, than most fruit juices – great news for chocoholics! On top of protecting the body from diseases and helping to prevent heart conditions, dark choco is a natural mood –booster.

EASY EATING TIP: Eat this healthy food in moderation – just one or two squares per day is enough to reap the benefits.

5. BONE BROTH

Bone broth is filled with nutrients and Forbes mentioned that it can be the superfood of tomorrow due to its nutritional benefits. There are some big companies that are investing a good amount of money in bone broths. Bone broth contains collagen which is good for your skin, hair, and joints. It also contains protein and vitamins such as vitamin A and vitamin K.

Benefits:

- Relaxes Muscles
- Relief from Joint Pain
- Removes Wrinkles
- Good for Skin
- Good for your Hair

6. DATES

Dates are a good source of natural sugar, due to this people think it can be dangerous for them but it's not the case. Dates are filled with nutrients that can give you plenty of energy boost. Arabs use this as a regular part of their diet. Dates are rich in protein, vitamin B-6, iron, magnesium, and potassium. Dates are high in polyphenols that help with inflammation.

Benefits:

- You will feel fuller
- Good source of Vitamin and iron
- Contains a high amount of polyphenols

This list can go on a long way, as there are many other healthiest foods out there. I pointed out some of those that top my list of healthiest foods and are easy to find and cheap. Anyone can find these foods in their local supermart.

7. BEETS

Good for the brain and skilled at lowering blood pressure, the humble beet is often overlooked as one of the healthiest foods on earth. The brightly-colored root vegetable is filled with folate magnesium and vitamin C. A good source of Nitric Oxide which helps with blood circulation. Beet punch is readily available at supermarkets.

EASY EATING TIP: Grate them into salads for a sweet, crunchy boost.

8. AVOCADO

Eating just one or two avocados a week gives you all the benefit of healthy monounsaturated fats, Vitamin B6 and loads of folate. Readily available all year round.

9. RASPBERRIES

Like most berries, raspberries are filled with antioxidants, to help keep the body healthy and free of disease. Fresh or frozen, they also provide Vitamin C, calcium and iron.

10. **GARLIC**

This pungent bulb has been used to ward off disease for centuries, as it inhibits the growth of bacteria, lowers cholesterol and blood pressure and has some serious anti-inflammatory power.

EASY EATING TIP: Crush it and cook it. Garlic tastes great in everything from dressings and sauces to curries and soups although the best benefits comes from raw garlic. Crush three to four cloves of raw garlic and leave for 15 minutes. Then cut up or grate garlic and mix with a tablespoon of honey. Tastes great and excellent for your health.

11. **LEMONS**

Often touted as the world's healthiest food, lemons have strong anti-inflammatory qualities and can help to inhibit the growth of cancer cells. They also have just as much Vitamin C as oranges.

12. **LENTILS**

Last but not least, this mighty legume is high in fiber and protein and adds great taste and texture to any meal. Vegans and vegetarians are often a fan of using lentils as a meat substitute in traditional recipes.

13. CELERY

One of the most nutritious herb around. Apart from using it as a food seasoning you can osterise and add about 2 tablespoons to a glassful of beet punch. Great for heart health.

3

TOP 10 SIMPLE AND NATURAL WAYS TO BOOST YOUR IMMUNE SYSTEM

By Linda B. White, MD

According to the Centers for Disease Control, influenza viruses continue to wreak misery in 41 states. Got your flu shot? Good, do it again next year.

However, keep in mind that other viruses cause respiratory illness: parainfluenza viruses, adenoviruses, coronaviruses, rhinoviruses....not to mention bacteria such as Streptococcus.

Despite the fact that your world teams with infectious microorganisms, most of the time, you're reasonable healthy, right? Thank your immune system, which defends you from disease-causing microbes. Now, step beyond gratitude to optimize the function of that system.

1. **Get enough sleep and manage stress.**
    Sleep deprivation and stress overload increase the hormone cortisol, prolonged elevation of which suppresses immune function.

2. **Avoid tobacco smoke.**
    It undermines basic immune defenses and raises the risk of bronchitis and pneumonia in everyone, and middle ear infections in kids.

3. **Drink less alcohol.**
    Excessive consumption impairs the immune system and increases vulnerability to lung infections.

4. **Eat plenty of vegetables, fruits, nuts, and seeds.**

Which will provide your body with the nutrients your immune system needs. A study in older adults showed that boosting fruit and vegetable intake improved antibody response to the Pneumovax vaccine, which protects against Streptococcus pneumonia.

5. Consider Probiotics.

Studies indicate supplements reduce the incidence of respiratory and gastrointestinal infections. Fermented milk products e.g. yogurt have also been shown to reduce respiratory infections in adults and kids.

6. Catch some rays.

Sunlight triggers the skin's production of vitamin D. In the summer, a 10-15 minute exposure (minus sunscreen) is enough. However, above 42 degrees latitude (Boston) from November through February, sunlight is too feeble and few foods contain this vitamin. Low vitamin D levels correlate with a greater risk of respiratory infection. A 2010 study in kids showed that 1200 IU a day of supplemental vitamin D reduced the risk of influenza A. However, a 2012 study that involved supplementing adults with colon cancer with 1000 IU a day failed to demonstrate protection against upper respiratory infections.

7. Go for the garlic.

Garlic is a broad-spectrum antimicrobial agent and immune booster. Because heat deactivates a key active ingredient, add it to foods just before serving.

8. Eat medicinal mushrooms.

Eat medicinal mushrooms such as shiitake and maitake (sometimes sold as "hen of the woods"). A recent study showed that a concentrated extract of shiitake enhanced immune function in women with breast cancer.

9. Try immune-supportive herbs.

If you get recurrent infections, consider taking immune-supportive herbs such as eleuthero (Eleutherococcus senticocus), Asian ginseng (Panax ginseng), American ginseng (Panax quinquefolius), or astragalus (A. membranaceus).

10. Make an echinacea tincture.

This is good to have on hand when respiratory viruses overwhelm your defenses. Recipe adapted from 500 TIME-TESTED HOME REMEDIES AND THE SCIENCE BEHIND THEM.

To a pint jar add 1 cup ground root of Echinacea purpurea root, a species shown to enhance immune function and moderately reduce cold symptom severity and duration. Add 1½ cup vodka and stir. If there isn't 1 to 2 inches of vodka layered above the ground root, add more vodka. Shake daily.After 4 weeks, strain through cheesecloth into a clean jar.At the first sniffle, take ½ teaspoon of tincture diluted in water every two hours while awake. After two days, reduce the dosage to ½ teaspoon 3 times a day for the duration of the cold.

4

COUNT YOUR BLESSINGS

Sometimes, though very rarely, happiness comes to us with a big bang, but usually it is in small doses or it is a realisation of the good things we have going for us. If we bring these areas to mind often enough in spite of the trials we are undergoing, they could cheer us up and remind us that in spite of everything, most of the time, we have a lot to be thankful for. Given below is a list of those happiness areas which we could do well to remember, if and when they apply to us. The list is long, but read it and see how much we may have going for us.

1. Peace in the country in which we live.
2. Peace in the home.
3. A compatible and caring mate.
4. A secure job or one you enjoy doing.
5. A regular salary.
6. A home
7. A car.
8. Good health – the absence of illness and the use and enjoyment of all our senses
9. Absence of pain.
10. An understanding boss.
11. Good friends.
12. A supportive family
13. Good weather.
14. Availability of good food.
15. Good living accommodations.
16. Satisfying sexual relations.
17. Availability of recreational facilities e.g. beaches, cinema, television, books, etc.
18. A good education

19. A shoulder to cry on
20. Someone to hug you, when you need one.
21. A sympathetic ear.
22. Good neighbours.
23. Absence of strife.
24. Availability of educational facilities.
25. Facilities that work e.g. electricity, telephone, internet (information and games at your fingertips).
26. Being able to afford essentials.
27. Being able to afford luxuries.
28. Protection from the criminal elements in society.
29. Redress for wrongdoings against you.
30. Absence of accidents
31. Absence of life threatening situations.
32. Well-behaved children
33. Holidays – Christmas and Carnival.
34. Music
35. Beauty in all its forms.
36. Finding things when you want them.

While all these things may not apply to all of us all the time, there are enough of them that will apply to us that would bring us some measure of comfort and happiness when we bring them back to mind. So when things are a bit rough and you are going through a hard time, remind yourself of some of the positive things in your life. It may help. Count your blessings.

5

6 ESSENTIAL INGREDIENTS YOU NEED

L-citrulline
To support healthy blood pressure... promote sharper memory and focus... and rev up your sexual performance...

Beet Root Powder
To boost your energy and endurance, plus help you walk longer and think more quickly on your feet, and...

Hawthorne Berry
It will increase blood flow, support healthy circulation, and help you get even more benefits from l-citrulline and beet root powder.

Vitamin B12
Most people over 50 are deficient in this crucial, energizing nutrient. Your cells need B12 to increase nitric oxide levels... and your brain, nerves, and muscles need it to work.

Vitamin C
This powerful antioxidant is necessary for boosting nitric oxide. That's because it stimulates the activity of an enzyme vital for producing it in your body.

Magnesium
About 80% of us are deficient in this important mineral, yet it's needed to relax muscles in your arteries so blood flows more freely. It also promotes healthy heart rhythm and keeps calcium from building up in your joints, brain, and heart.

6

THE HAPPINESS CONCEPT

HOW YOU LIVE YOUR LIFE IS YOUR RESPONSIBILITY

We all have challenges and responsibilities. How we deal with them is key to achieving some measure of happiness in this life.

While other people play a role in your life, you are chiefly responsible for your own happiness. Self knowledge is very important. The more in-depth you know yourself, it is better for you. One of the best piece of advice I have come across is from Socrates who encouraged people to *"Examine your life."*

It's how you think that makes you happy. The more you know yourself the happier you can become, because you know what you have to deal with. It's being realistic. It's up to you to find the solutions to the problems in your life. Actively pursue finding those solutions. Learn to accept those situations for which there are obviously no solutions. Do the things you enjoy doing. Love yourself, spoil yourself sometimes.

While living a disciplined life is necessary both for ourselves and others, don't make yourself uncomfortable by following too rigid a regimen. Take a break. Fill your life with variety, interspace relaxing and variety.

Your beliefs make you. Believe that love is available. Believe that you are lovable.

LIVING YOUR LIFE

We all have a wide range of responsibilities that we must take care of if we are to survive in this world. Many of us accept and deal with them and achieve a good measure of success, comfort and happiness especially where it involves doing things we are comfortable with and enjoy.

To those whom these responsibilities become tedious or boring there are other areas which can be looked at which can make life interesting.

The following are some clues to achieving this: **VIFPAP.**

- **VARIETY**
  Seek out variety in your life. Do something different now and then.

- **INTEREST**
  Find out what really interest you in life and get active in those areas, hobbies, etc

- **FUN**
  Have fun. Play games, visit fun places, eat food that you really enjoy.

- **PROJECTS**
  Identify achievable projects and work on them

- **ACHIEVEMENTS**

Experience the pleasure you get from your achievements.

- **PEOPLE**

Surround yourself with people you get along with.

Seek out people who are nice to be with and spend time with them and keep communicating with them even if whatsapp is your only means. Also remember that staying healthy should be high on your list of priorities. That's why it is so important to have a healthy lifestyle.

7

THINGS YOU HAVE TO DO TO STAY HEALTHY

All of us should know of the saying 'One ounce of prevention is worth a pound of cure!' Is this telling us that there is a minimum requirement that we should observe if we are to stay healthy throughout our lives. I think so!

What is this requirement?

If we all knew this and kept it, most of us should be able to live long healthy happy lives. Basically, this could be identified as eating the right foods and exercising. Usually the experts go to the extreme in recommending these two requirements to the extent that we feel guilty about enjoying some delicious foods. I honestly feel that there is a middle path we can follow where we don't have to be fanatical or make ourselves miserable in order to stay healthy. We should be able to enjoy delectable snacks e.g. ice-cream, chocolate and fast foods now and then.

We need energy to work so we must consume some carbohydrates. It's the excess that damages our bodies e.g. too much rice, bread, sugar and salt. While we need these foods we need always to manage/minimise their intake if we are to stay healthy. At the same time, we need to consume enough protein foods and vitamins to support our strength and vital processes of our bodies. Predominantly this means eating lean meat, fruits, vegetables and nuts and taking a good multivitamin supplement. The key is we should make healthy foods our main source of nutrition.

What about exercise, that's the last thing some folks want to do BUT if we are physically active life, that will help. Some of us lead pretty active lives in which our work involves a good deal of physical activity. Formal exercise applies to people who live sedentary lives e.g. those who work in offices where they have to sit all day e.g. cashiers, computer operators etc. Such people should include some form of exercise in their lives even if it is walking.

If you like exercising, go ahead! If you don't, take a regular walk about three times a week. If you can take a sea bath and get some sun in the process to get the free vitamin D so essential for our good health.

If for whatever reason you are a stay at home, remember that sitting and lying down too long are definitely things we should avoid.

The key is moderation. Balance and moderation are the key in achieving a happy, healthy life. You can also visit my website www.awebsage.com for more assistance in pursuing the good life!

8

THE HEALTHY LIFESTYLE

The rules for having a healthy body are surprisingly simple compared to the boatloads of conflicting information you can find on the internet. Medical doctors have one idea, chiropractors have another, and naturopaths many more ideas.

Today, we are taught to expect health to come in a pill. The simplicity of the truth is simplicity.

THE SIMPLE TRUTH
Most often, the truth is simple. So, here goes the truth, from least to most important:

TAKE SUPPLEMENTS WEEKLY
If you need a supplement, don't take it every day; the body becomes resistant to anything we do daily. Weekly supplements are much more effective. If you have a nutrient or herb to treat an illness or health problem, then daily might be needed, for a time, but usually after 90 days it isn't effective anyway, and, if continued, can be changed to weekly.

EXERCISE REGULARLY
This doesn't mean daily. Do interval exercises for at least 20 minutes 3 days per week.

EAT GOOD FOOD
Avoid processed foods like sugar and flour. Limit restaurant food and cook food yourself. Eat whole foods. Occasionally eating out, having a dessert, or

eating ice cream on a hot summer day is not the issue. It's what you eat daily that matters.

SLEEP AT 10PM

The deep sleep we get between 10pm and 2am allows the proper release of Growth Hormone (HGH) which is important for repairing the body. Also, be sure you go to bed with an empty stomach, which also releases HGH *(Don't eat after 6pm)*.

STRESS REDUCTION

Stress will destroy any great lifestyle program. The greatest anti-stress program is faith, hope, and love. These three will remove anxiety, depression, and allow you to have a happy, stress-free life even if storms are raging around you.

FAST PERIODICALLY

Fasting has been touted as the best way to maintain perfect weight.

If you do these things, it will assist greatly in keeping you healthy and happy.

9

10 WAYS TO LOVE YOURSELF!

How to love yourself?

HERE ARE A FEW IDEAS

APPRECIATE YOUR OWN COMPANY

We love our family and friends, and in some ways, we can measure our wealth and good fortune by how many we have of both but sometimes we need reminding that we can be our own good company...

Some of us can barely squeeze in ten minutes for a soak in bath and that's fine. For others an afternoon of solitude without even the distraction of a Booker movie can do wonders to soothe the soul and get us back in touch with the sound of our own heartbeat. And for the lucky few who can manage a weekend retreat, a solitary walk or sunup-to-sundown away from it all..... ahhh, bliss!

LEARN A NEW SKILL

You stand there admiring a painting but have you ever picked up a brush? You can't get enough of your favorite author but when last did you commit your thoughts to a paper? Who me, you say? Yes, you!

Learn to do something you never thought you'd be good at. You'll be surprised when you discover a new aptitude. And the great thing about the electronic age is that often you don't have to leave your house to take a class (except maybe for hang-gliding).

Your next teacher might be just a few clicks away ..

CUT OUT THE MAUVAIS-LANGUE

You've probably never been as mean, sarcastic and insulting to another human being as you are routinely to yourself. "I suck at this, I hate myself when.. I look terrible!" Don't you think you beat yourself up enough? Replace negative self-chat with a sweet, sincere compliment every once in a while. It will do you a world of good.

FEED YOURSELF BETTER

You wouldn't give your dog have the garbage you put into your mouth: pesticide-laden, artificially grown, sugar loaded, over processed... ick,ick and ick! Treat yourself a detox weekend eating only fresh natural products. Try to hang on to at least one healthy habit you picked up.

Feel your body say, aahh!

PACK YOURSELF OFF TO BED EARLY

Once in a while, forget the late night movie, put down the book, make your excuses to lovers, family, friends and anyone else who might be encouraging you to stay up late. Exchange it for the revolutionary technique:

STEP ONE: Dive under the covers!
STEP TWO: Stay there!

STOP YEARNING FOR THE NEIGHBORS GREEN GRASS

Don't envy what others own or what they have achieved. You don't know what they did to get there. Besides, they're them and you're you. Look down at your own feet and admire the lovely green grass growing under them.

Then mow the lawn..... KIDDING!

CLEAN UP AS YOU'RE EXPECTING COMPANY...

Okay, maybe this one involves hard work but does your house only get spiffed up when someone's coming over?

Even if it's just for a few hours, declare war on dirt, murder a few dust bunnies and put some flowers on the table. Then lay out a dinner treat for your most important dinner guest, YOU!

SMILE MORE...

When you smile your brain releases happy hormones that make you feel better even if you have nothing to smile about.
It's a simple equation;

Those who smile more live happier lives.

Yeah it's that easy!

FORGIVE YOURSELF...

The lord himself promised to forgive us as we forgive others but as hard as it is sometimes to forgive others for their wrongdoings, it doubly difficult to let go of our sins. Instead we chew on them like yesterday's gum even though it's hard, bitter, and tasteless.

Spit it out fast before you choke on it...

LOVE SOMEONE ELSE....

Love is the world's greatest perpetual motion machine. It bounces endlessly back and forth between you and everyone else. It slows down sometimes and speeds up others but its always moving.

Give love, radiate it, pass it on unselfishly and it will always, always, come back to you!

10

THE TEN MINUTE WORKOUT

This workout is a combination of High Intensity Interval training (HIIT), strength, yoga, and dynamic tension. All these exercise should be done slowly and gently.

1. Standing up straight swing your outstretched arms alternately in a circular motion ten times around. Then swing them in the opposite direction ten times around. Repeat. In all you would have swung your arms 40 times around, ten times in each direction.

2. Pushups. Do any amount of pushups that you can do comfortably up to 20. If you are new to pushups you can do them with your knees on the ground rather than your toes. It is less strenuous that way.

3. Stoop with your bottom close to your heels and clasp your arms in front of you as if in prayer. Hold that position for the count of 100.

4. In that same stooping position lean over to the left supporting yourself with both hands on the ground in front of the left leg. Your legs should be opened wide enough so you can lean over comfortably to one side and then to the other while supporting yourself with your hands to the left and to the right. You will end up doing a gentle rocking motion from side to side. Do this rocking motion ten times on each side.

5. Stand up and bend forward from the waist keeping your upper body as straight as possible and parallel to the floor. In this position stretch out your arms and clasp your hands together. Hold this pose for as long as you can for the count of between 50 and 100. Slowly stand up straight and stretch each arm straight up upwards slowly once on each side. This is an excellent exercise for strengthening the back and preventing lower back pain.

6. Squat.
There are two ways you can do this.
   - Version 1. You can simple stoop till you thighs are parallel to the ground for ten times.
   - Version 2. Spread your legs far apart and bend to each side as low as you can comfortably go. Do as many as you can comfortably do.
7. Stand up straight and pull in your stomach as far as you can twenty times. Breathe out as you suck in your gut. (Don't forget to breathe in...hmmm).
8. Contract as many of your muscles one by one as many time as you feel comfortably.....biceps, triceps, chest, back, thighs, calves.

End of workout

Take your time. You don't have to do all of them all of the time, although together they only take about ten minutes and you only need to do them 3 times a week. If you find that this is too much to do, just make sure you do some sort of exercise about 3 times weekly. Many people replace formal exercising by walking about 30 minutes three times a week. To your fantastic health.

Anthony Webster *10/4/2021*